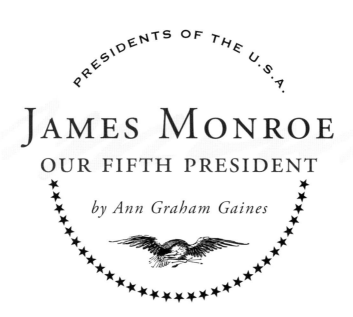

PRESIDENTS OF THE U.S.A.

JAMES MONROE
OUR FIFTH PRESIDENT

by Ann Graham Gaines

THE CHILD'S WORLD®

Published in the United States of America

The Child's World®
1980 Lookout Drive • Mankato, MN 56003-1705
800-599-READ • www.childsworld.com

Acknowledgments
The Child's World®: Mary Berendes, Publishing Director

The Creative Spark: Mary McGavic, Project Director and Page Production;
Shari Joffe, Editorial Director; Deborah Goodsite, Photo Research

The Design Lab: Kathleen Petelinsek, Design

Content Adviser: Meghan C. Budinger, Assistant Director & Curator, James
Monroe Museum and Memorial Library, Fredericksburg, Virginia

Photos
Cover and page 3: The Granger Collection, New York

Interior: Alamy: 7 (North Wind Picture Archives), 8 (brt PHOTO), 12 (Andre
Jenny); The Art Archive: 18, 19 (Chateau de Blerancourt/Gianni Dagli Orti); Art
Resource, NY: 14 and 38 (National Portrait Gallery, Smithsonian Institution),
28 (Scala); The Bridgeman Art Library: 4, 30 (Private Collection/Peter Newark
American Pictures), 23 (American Antiquarian Society, Worcester, Massachusetts,
USA), 34 (Collection of the New-York Historical Society, USA); Corbis: 32 and
39 (Bettmann); Courtesy of Ash Lawn-Highland, Charlottesville, VA: 10, 35;
Courtesy of the James Monroe Museum & Memorial Library, Fredericksburg, VA
(JM76.004): 37; Getty Images: 15 (Imagno), 17 (MPI), 36 (Victor R. Boswell,
Jr./National Geographic); The Granger Collection, New York: 5, 24, 31; iStock-
photo: 44 (Tim Fan); Library of Congress: 25, 27 and 38; North Wind Picture
Archives: 21 (North Wind); SuperStock: 9 (Huntington Library), 20 (SuperStock,
Inc.); U.S. Air Force photo: 45; Virginia Department of Historic Resources: 33.

Library of Congress Cataloging-in-Publication Data
Gaines, Ann.
  James Monroe / by Ann Graham Gaines.
     p. cm. — (Presidents of the U.S.A.)
  Includes bibliographical references and index.
  ISBN 978-1-60253-034-8 (library bound : alk. paper)
  1. Monroe, James, 1758–1831—Juvenile literature. 2. Presidents—United
States—Biography—Juvenile literature. I. Title.
  E372.G349 2008
  973.5'4092—dc22
  [B]
                          2007042610

Thomas Jefferson once said James Monroe (above) was so honest that "if you turned his soul inside out there would not be a spot on it."

TABLE OF CONTENTS

CHAPTER ONE

A START IN POLITICS

When James Monroe became the fifth president of the United States, he already had a lot of political experience. He had been a member of Virginia's state **legislature,** the Continental Congress, and the U.S. Senate. He had been elected governor of Virginia four times. He had served as a **diplomat** in France and Great Britain. These jobs helped prepare him to be president. As president, he helped the country expand its borders. It was also during his presidency that Americans began to talk seriously about how to deal with the issue of slavery.

James Monroe was born on April 28, 1758. He was the son of Spence and Elizabeth Monroe. The Monroe family owned a farm in Westmoreland County, Virginia. At that time, Virginia was still a British colony, one of thirteen in North America.

James Monroe served as president from 1817 to 1825.

Spence and Elizabeth Monroe had five children together. Like his father and grandfather, Spence Monroe earned his living growing tobacco. He owned a small **plantation.** African American slaves grew the crops in his fields and worked in his house.

When he was very young, James Monroe learned all his lessons from his mother and father. He did not go to school until he was 11 years old. Then he became a student at Campbelltown Academy, a fine school in Virginia. His teacher had also taught George Washington many years before.

The four men who were president before James Monroe were old enough to remember life in the

James Monroe was born on this farm in Westmoreland County, Virginia.

colonies before the American **Revolution.** Monroe, however, was too young to recall peaceful times. From a very early age, he heard people talk about a **rebellion.** In the 1760s, England began to make the American colonists pay **taxes.** Colonists such as Spence Monroe and his friends thought this was unfair. They believed Britain should not tax the colonists because they would not let them have a **representative** in the government. The colonists discussed ways to make England see their point of view. But eventually, they would have to fight for their freedom.

George Washington and Spence Monroe were friends. When James was a little boy, Washington visited the Monroes' farm.

In 1774, just one year before the American Revolution began, James Monroe stopped going to school. Spence Monroe had died, and James was the family's oldest son. This meant he **inherited** his father's estate. The estate included all of his father's money and land. Because James was still a teenager, his Uncle Joseph helped him make decisions about running the farm.

James stayed at home for a time. But soon he moved to Virginia's capital city, Williamsburg. He attended the College of William and Mary. There he studied Latin, Greek, literature, math, and science.

In April of 1775, British soldiers came to Williamsburg. The people of the city had been gathering guns and other supplies. They were preparing for war against England. The British soldiers tried to take away the colonists' weapons. This made Monroe so angry that he joined a **militia.** He wanted to help the rebellion in any way he could. His company of

volunteer soldiers drilled every day, practicing marching and shooting their guns.

In the spring of 1776, Virginians formed a new regiment and joined the Continental Army. This was the American colonists' army, commanded by General George Washington. James Monroe decided to leave college and sign up. In June, he and other soldiers seized British supplies of guns and **ammunition** left behind when the British governor fled Virginia. He was **promoted** to lieutenant for his bravery.

On July 4, 1776, the American colonies declared their independence from England. That September, the Virginians were sent to fight with the army in New

Monroe traveled to Williamsburg, the capital city of Virginia, in 1774. He went there to attend the College of William and Mary, shown here. In 1776, he left school to join the army. He wanted to help the United States win its independence.

Boats carrying American soldiers crossed the Delaware River all through Christmas night of 1776. General Washington (standing at left) had planned a surprise attack on the enemy. Monroe was one of the first soldiers to cross the Delaware that night.

York. Monroe was at the Battle of Harlem Heights and the Battle of White Plains. He also distinguished himself in the Battle of Trenton. This battle began on Christmas night in 1776. Both armies had settled down into winter quarters. General Washington decided to surprise the enemy. In the middle of the night, American soldiers sneaked across the Delaware River. As part of a scouting party that was to spy on enemy forces, James Monroe was one of the first soldiers to cross the river. The next day, Washington's forces attacked!

During the battle that followed, Monroe fought bravely and showed tremendous leadership skills. Both he and his commander were wounded. Washington promoted Monroe again. He even wrote to Congress to tell them how brave Monroe had been. Washington ended his letter by saying he wished "we had one thousand officers like him."

Monroe had to rest after he was wounded, but he went back to the army in the spring of 1777. He took part in the Battle of Brandywine. He spent one terrible winter with the army at Valley Forge. He fought at the Battle of Monmouth. In 1780, he decided to leave the army. By this time, he was the aide, or assistant, to a general. He found this frustrating. He wanted a command of his own. When he could not have one, he decided the time had come to return to his studies. Now he wanted to study law.

Back in Williamsburg, Monroe met the governor of Virginia, Thomas Jefferson. The two men formed a close friendship. Jefferson would be Monroe's friend

Monroe was the last of the presidents to have been an adult during the Revolutionary War. In fact, he was one of only two presidents to have served in the war. The other was George Washington.

After he fought in the Revolutionary War, Monroe served as an assistant to Virginia's governor, Thomas Jefferson (above).

and **mentor** for years to come. Monroe was appointed one of Jefferson's clerks. He also took lessons in law from Jefferson. At that time, there were no special law schools.

By the time the war ended in 1781, Monroe had become interested in **politics.** Some of his friends asked him to run for the Virginia legislature. He won the election.   One year later, he was

James Monroe was a tall man. He stood more than six feet tall.

Elizabeth Kortright and James Monroe were married in February of 1786. Elizabeth was a charming and beautiful woman. In the 1790s, when the Monroes lived in Paris, the French called Elizabeth la belle Américaine— *"the beautiful American."*

elected to the United States Congress, which met in Philadelphia. There he helped write laws for the new country.

In 1785, New York became the capital of the United States, and Congress was moved there. In New York, Monroe met a beautiful, quiet woman named Elizabeth Kortright. They married the next year. When Monroe's **term** in Congress ended, he and Elizabeth went to live in Fredericksburg, Virginia. Monroe began working as a lawyer.

In 1787, an important **convention** was held in Philadelphia. Every state sent **delegates** to help write a new **constitution.** It would describe how the country's new government would work. Monroe was disappointed when he wasn't chosen to represent Virginia at the Constitutional Convention.

After the members of the convention finished writing the Constitution, Americans had to approve it. Each state held another convention where representatives voted whether to ratify, or accept, the Constitution. Monroe attended the Virginia Ratifying Convention, where he voted against the Constitution. He did not like it because it took away power from states and gave it to the federal government. Most Americans did not agree with Monroe. They thought it was a good idea for the national government to be strong. Finally, enough states ratified the Constitution.

When he was at college, Monroe had a complaint that many students shared—he signed a petition protesting the awful food served there.

HIGHLAND

In 1793, Monroe bought a large piece of land near Thomas Jefferson's home. There he planned to build a beautiful home and establish a farm. Monroe hoped to live at his plantation, called Highland, immediately after he purchased it. He wanted to farm and to be closer to his good friend Thomas Jefferson. But soon after Monroe bought Highland, the U.S. government sent Monroe to France as a diplomat.

Monroe and his family did not move to the plantation until 1799, six years after he bought the land. At first, Monroe's home there was just a simple wooden house. But over a 16-year period, Monroe added buildings and gardens. It's possible that his good friend Thomas Jefferson, who designed and built his own house, made helpful suggestions about the design of the plantation.

The Monroes frequently had to leave Highland because of James's career. Still, they considered it their home for more than 25 years. During his two terms as president, Monroe often talked of retiring there.

Unfortunately, the Monroes had to sell Highland in 1826. They did not have enough money to run the farm. The next owner called it Ash Lawn. Today Monroe's plantation has become a museum. It is known as Ash Lawn–Highland. Visitors can tour the mansion and learn more about President Monroe.

CHAPTER TWO

LIFE AS A DIPLOMAT

When the Constitution was approved in 1789, a new American government formed. The country elected its first president, George Washington. James Monroe had known Washington for years. He believed he would make a great leader.

Monroe wanted to be a part of the new government, too. In 1790, he ran for and was elected to the U.S. Senate. During Washington's presidency, two **political parties** formed. With his friends Thomas Jefferson and James Madison, Monroe helped establish the Republican Party. At that time, it was also called the Democratic-Republican Party. Its members believed that ordinary citizens should be able to play a role in their government. Their opponents belonged to the Federalist Party. They believed only rich, well-educated men should run the country. For many years to come, the Democratic-Republicans and the Federalists would have many disagreements about how the new nation should be run.

In 1794, President George Washington asked Monroe to leave the Senate and become a diplomat. Washington knew that Monroe sometimes disagreed

In France, Elizabeth Monroe rescued the wife of the Marquis de Lafayette. The Marquis was a wealthy Frenchman who had traveled to America years before to fight in the Revolution. Poor French people had since begun their own revolution. They were angry that rich people had all the power in France, so they threatened to kill many of them. Madame Lafayette was imprisoned, but Mrs. Monroe helped her escape.

with him, but he admired his independent thinking. So he asked him to become the United States' representative to France. At that time, France was fighting a war against England. The United States was trying to **negotiate** a **treaty** with England. This placed Monroe in a tricky situation.

James, Elizabeth, and their daughter Eliza went to live in Paris, France's capital city. French officials were not friendly to Monroe at first. They knew that some Americans wanted the United States to become an English **ally.** England was France's enemy. But Monroe soon became well liked. One reason was that he respected the French for having fought their own revolution. Before he arrived, the people of France had overthrown their king and created a new **democracy.**

James and Elizabeth Monroe loved France. They thought it was a beautiful country. They liked the French people, their language, their art, and their way of life. The Monroes learned to speak French. Unfortunately, the fact that Monroe liked France and its people became a problem. Members of the Federalist Party thought Monroe was too friendly with the French. Washington wanted the United States to be **neutral.** He didn't want to take sides with either England or France.

Finally, Washington gave in to the Federalists. He ordered Monroe to come home. "I was charged with

*Monroe served as U.S. **minister** to France for two years. He and his wife thought Paris (left) was a beautiful city and they enjoyed their time there.*

After the decision was made to fire Monroe from his post in France, **Secretary of State** Timothy Pickering waited six weeks before writing to tell him. An election was coming up. Pickering wanted John Adams to become the second president, not his opponent, Thomas Jefferson. He delayed writing to Monroe so that Monroe would arrive in the United States after the election—too late to help Jefferson beat Adams.

James and Elizabeth Monroe often spoke French to each other in private even after they returned to the United States.

a failure to perform my duty," Monroe later remembered. He felt he was being punished for something he didn't do, and this made him angry.

Back in Virginia, he gave some attention to his plantation and his law practice. But he spent most of his time writing a booklet about what had happened in France. It was titled *A View of the Conduct of the Executive, in the **Foreign Affairs** of the United States.* He wanted to show the public that he had done a good job. He said he had always tried to do what was best for his country. He even said that President Washington was making bad decisions about how to deal with other nations.

When Monroe's paper was published, Federalists were sure he could never be elected to office again. After all, Americans truly admired President Washington, and Monroe had said negative things about him. But Virginia voters still supported James Monroe. Thomas Jefferson assured him that one day, he would get back into politics.

In December of 1799, Monroe ran for governor of Virginia. He was so popular that no one ran against him. He was re-elected in 1800 and 1801. While he was governor, he improved the state's tax system, the courts, and the militia. The state house was built, as well as many schools and hospitals. By the end of Monroe's third term, Thomas Jefferson had been elected the third president of the United States. Jefferson asked Monroe to go back to France on a special **mission.**

THE LOUISIANA PURCHASE
MESSRS. MONROE AND LIVINGSTONE COMPLETING NEGOTIATIONS WITH TALLYRAND, APRIL 30, 1803

France controlled both the city of New Orleans and the Mississippi River. Jefferson hoped Monroe could convince the French to sell New Orleans to the United States. He also wanted France to keep allowing Americans to sail their ships on the Mississippi, which made it much easier to transport goods from one place to another. The American representative in France, Robert R. Livingston, had not been able to get the French to agree to these requests. Monroe did not know if he could, either.

Monroe was in for a surprise. When he arrived in Paris, the French had just asked Livingston if the

James Monroe (center) and Robert Livingston (left) negotiated the Louisiana Purchase with a French official named Charles Talleyrand. Monroe and Livingston were thrilled to learn that France would sell not just New Orleans, but the entire Louisiana Territory.

The Louisiana Purchase gave the United States 530,000 acres (800,000 square miles) for just $15 million—about 4 cents per acre. This painting shows the French raising their flag in New Orleans for the last time before handing the territory over to the United States.

United States would like to buy not just New Orleans, but the whole Louisiana Territory. This was a huge piece of land. But Monroe and Livingston had no way to ask President Jefferson quickly whether this was a good idea. It took many weeks for letters to travel across the Atlantic Ocean in those days. So Monroe and Livingston did what they thought was best. They agreed to France's offer. For $15 million, they bought Louisiana. It included enough land to double the size of the United States.

Americans were happy when they found out about the Louisiana Purchase. It made Monroe a hero. Jefferson sent him on other missions in England and then Spain. These were difficult times in Europe because France had a new ruler. Napoleon was starting wars all over the continent. He wanted to control all of Europe. Monroe was not able to build friendships with either England or Spain. Their leaders had no time to talk about their relationships with the United States. All they could think about was the threat of Napoleon.

From France, Monroe returned to Virginia. Once more he got involved in state politics. He was elected to the Virginia legislature in 1810. Then in 1811, he became governor of the state for the fourth time. The very same year, President James Madison asked Monroe to become his secretary of state. His job would be to help the United States in its relations with other countries. Madison knew that Monroe had a lot of experience with foreign affairs. Even so, this would be a difficult job. For one thing, England kept causing trouble for the United States. The British wanted to stop Americans from selling their goods in

President James Madison (above), impressed with Monroe's diplomatic skills and experience, asked Monroe to be his secretary of state.

On August 19, 1812, the U.S.S. Constitution *battled and captured the British ship* Guerriére. *It was the first ship-to-ship victory for the U.S. Navy during the War of 1812.*

Europe. So the British navy kept American ships from sailing to Europe by attacking them at sea.

For a time, Madison and Monroe tried to avoid another war with England. Finally, they realized that it was the only way to make England leave the United States alone. On June 18, 1812, America declared war. With that, the War of 1812 began. If the United States did not win, it risked losing its independence.

THE LOUISIANA PURCHASE

James Monroe went to France for the second time on a special mission during Thomas Jefferson's presidency. There Monroe helped negotiate the purchase of the Louisiana Territory, which allowed the United States to take over what the French called la Louisiane. This was a huge colony that included all the lands along the Mississippi River. President Jefferson was so excited about the Louisiana Purchase that he sent explorers Meriwether Lewis and William Clark out into the region to find out just what the United States had gained.

Over the years, the Louisiana Territory became the states of Arkansas, Missouri, Iowa, Oklahoma, Nebraska, Kansas, and South Dakota, plus parts of Louisiana, North Dakota, Minnesota, Colorado, New Mexico, Texas, Wyoming, and Montana. James Monroe had helped the United States increase in size by 800,000 square miles.

CHAPTER THREE

BLESSED WITH PEACE

When the War of 1812 broke out between the United States and England, James Monroe held a very important job. As secretary of state, he was very involved in decisions about how the United States would fight the war.

For a long time, it looked as if Americans could not win the war. By the end of August of 1814, British soldiers had attacked Washington, D.C. They even set the Capitol and the presidential mansion on fire.

Throughout the war, President Madison depended on Monroe for advice. After the British burned Washington, Secretary of War John Armstrong resigned. Madison asked Monroe to take over as secretary of war. He remained the secretary of state as well. He had a lot of responsibilities. Monroe later wrote about what happened when he took charge of the war. He remembered how the capital city "was still smoking, its public buildings in ruins. . . .For the first month at least, I never went to bed." He had to work even in the middle of the night.

With or without sleep, Monroe did his job well. With him in charge, the Americans began to win

Stop, Stop, Stop Brother Jonathan, or I shall fall with the loss of Blood — I thought to have been too heavy for you — But I must acknowledge your Superior skill — Two blows to my one! — And so well directed too! Mercy, mercy on me, how does this happen!!!

Ha—Ah Johnny! you thought yourself a Boxer did you! — I'll let you know we are an Enterprizing Nation, and ready to meet you with equal force any day.

A BOXING MATCH, or Another Bloody Nose for JOHN BULL.

When Monroe became secretary of war, the United States started to win more battles, especially at sea. This cartoon bragged about the American defeat of an English warship, the Boxer. *King George III of England and President Madison are shown in a boxing match. The king begs Madison to stop fighting. He even admits that the United States is stronger than England.*

more battles. The English people thought the war was costing too much money. After a time, their government agreed to stop fighting.

The United States did not really win the War of 1812 because its army had not truly beaten the British. But the British gave up and went home. At the end of the war, the United States had not lost any territory— or its independence—to Great Britain. In fact, Great Britain now respected the United States and let it travel the Atlantic Ocean freely. Americans were very proud.

Monroe's reputation as a smart man and a good leader grew during the war. When it was over, Monroe went back to working full-time as the secretary of state.

James Monroe wanted to join the army and fight in the War of 1812, but Madison needed him too much in Washington, D.C.

Monroe (right) helped Madison make important decisions during the War of 1812. Americans began to think Monroe could make an excellent president.

Then he worked on the treaty between the United States and England. He also began to negotiate with England to remove its navy ships from the Great Lakes.

In 1816, James Madison's term as president ended. James Monroe ran for the office. He won by a huge number of votes. In his **inaugural address,** he said how thankful he was to become president "when the United States are blessed with peace." Monroe took his oath of office in front of the Capitol building, which was still being restored. The presidential mansion also needed to be repaired before his family could move into it.

The period in which Monroe was president was called the "Era of Good Feeling." In many ways, it was a time when Americans were happy. The country enjoyed good fortune and was at peace. It also grew much larger.

One of Monroe's goals was to establish the nation's borders: two of its boundaries were in dispute. In 1818, John Quincy Adams, Monroe's secretary of state, settled a disagreement about the border between

Some Republicans did not want James Monroe to run for president in 1816 because he was from Virginia. There had already been three other presidents from that state. In the end, the party chose Monroe, who was more popular with the people than William Harris Crawford, the other Republican who might have run.

After the presidential mansion was burned by the British, only the walls remained. They were terribly blackened by the smoke. Workers restored the house and painted it white again.

James Monroe was not yet 60 when he became president. Even though he wasn't old, he seemed old-fashioned to many Americans. This was because he wore old-style clothing, including knee breeches. He also wore his hair in an old-fashioned ponytail.

James and Elizabeth Monroe's daughters were grown when their father was elected president. Still, it was a large Monroe family that moved into the White House. The Monroes' eldest daughter and her husband, one of Monroe's brothers, and Elizabeth's nephew all lived there.

the United States and Canada. At the same time, Spain still controlled much of Mexico. In 1819, Spain and the United States agreed on exactly where the Louisiana Territory ended and Mexico began.

Early in his presidency, Monroe faced one especially big problem. The territory of Missouri wanted to become a state. Some people there owned slaves. One congressman said that it should become a state only if its citizens agreed not to buy any new slaves. They also had to agree to let all the slaves go free at a certain point in the future. But southerners did not want Missouri to be a "free" state (a state where slavery was illegal). If it were free, then there would be fewer "slave states" than "free states." They were afraid this would mean the slave states would be less powerful. The free states might then make slavery illegal everywhere.

Congress would finally solve this problem with the Missouri **Compromise** of 1820. This decision let Missouri enter the Union as a slave state. At the same time, Maine entered as a free state. This kept the number of slave states and free states equal. Monroe signed the compromise on March 3, and Missouri became the 24th state.

Other states would soon be formed out of land the United States had received in the Louisiana Purchase. Years before, two **surveyors** had established a border between Pennsylvania and Maryland. The border was called the Mason-Dixon Line, in honor of the surveyors. The Compromise stretched this

imaginary line to the west into the Louisiana Territory. Slavery was now illegal in all new states north of that line. It would be legal in all the states south of it.

As more people began to believe slavery was wrong, the Mason-Dixon Line would come to symbolize the boundary between slavery and freedom. The Missouri Compromise had created bitterness between Americans. But many believed Monroe and the U.S. Congress had done a good job of keeping things fair.

Artist John Reubens Smith created this painting of the U.S. Capitol after it was restored from the fire of 1814. Washington, D.C., was very different when Monroe was president. It was still a rural area. Cows even grazed in the area now called the Mall.

THE AMERICAN WEST

The American West always fascinated James Monroe. When he first joined Congress, he often talked about what he thought should happen with the lands the United States owned in and around Ohio. At the time, that was the nation's "far West." But after Monroe helped negotiate the Louisiana Purchase, the nation stretched much, much farther. Americans started to move west right away. By 1810, 1.4 million U.S. citizens lived in the Mississippi River Valley. Over the next 10 years, another million people moved there.

By that time, "mountain men" had begun to go into the Rocky Mountains to trap animals for their fur. One of them, John Colter, discovered the area now known as Yellowstone National Park. Army Captain Stephen Long led a group of soldiers and scientists across the Great Plains and into the Rocky Mountains. They went there on orders from President Monroe. He realized that many more Americans would soon be moving to the West, and he wanted to know what the region was like.

CHAPTER FOUR

A WORLD POWER

The issue of slavery occupied a great deal of President James Monroe's attention during his first term. And yet he is remembered most for helping the United States become a world power. During his presidency, the nation increased greatly in size. It also gained a bigger voice in what would happen in the world.

The expeditions James Monroe sent out determined how far the nation stretched across the continent. But Monroe didn't just figure out how big the nation was. He also helped the United States grow even bigger. He pushed the nation's frontier 1,500 miles farther west to the Yellowstone River. He also helped the country gain a large part of Florida.

Back in 1812, the United States had taken over the Spanish territory of West Florida. Spain was angry, but it did not fight to get the land back. The area became a territory of the United States. By 1818, problems began in East Florida, which Spain still controlled. Seminoles and other Native Americans who lived there felt great anger toward American settlers, who had been taking land away from their people in Georgia. To fight back,

In 1818, President Monroe sent General Andrew Jackson (seated) to Georgia, where Native Americans were attacking U.S. settlers. Jackson and his troops then crossed the border into Florida. They seized Spanish territory there. Jackson did this without orders from the U.S. government.

Seminoles from Florida began to cross into Georgia and attack the settlers. Monroe sent General Andrew Jackson and his troops there to stop them.

Jackson wanted to do more than just stop the Seminole attacks. He wanted to take over East Florida as well, making it part of the nation's territory. He did not wait for orders from Monroe or Congress, but marched his soldiers into the region. There they fought the Seminoles and captured Spanish forts.

Florida came under American rule, although Jackson had acted without permission from the government.

Monroe did not like what Jackson had done, but he took advantage of it. He realized officials in Spain did not want more trouble. In the Adams-Onís Treaty, the United States and Spain agreed that East Florida would become part of the United States. Spain agreed never to try to take back any part of Florida.

The treaty also established the southern boundary of the United States, west of the Mississippi River. The United States gave up claims it had made on Texas. It also agreed to pay $5 million of Spanish **debt.**

Five states were added to the Union while Monroe was president. Only one president had more. That was Benjamin Harrison, who had six.

When James Monroe ran for president the second time, he was unopposed.

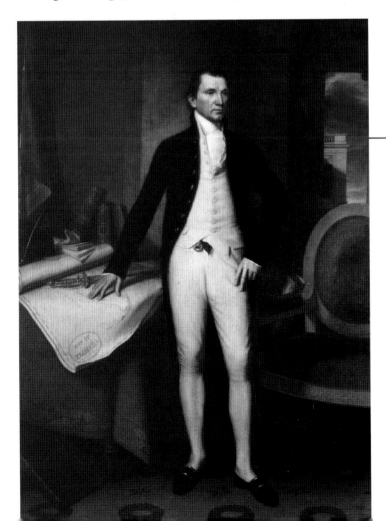

President Monroe (left) did not approve of Jackson's actions in Florida. After all, Jackson had seized the territory without permission from the government. But many Americans were happy that the United States now controlled all of Florida.

The election of 1816 was the last time the Federalists were still an important political party in the United States. The party fell apart soon afterward.

When Monroe ran for president in 1820, he won 231 out of 232 electoral votes. George Washington is the only president to have won every electoral vote.

Monroe was reelected in 1820. Americans thought he was a great president. He won by a **landslide.** He had some problems in his second term, however. One problem arose after a bank loaned him a large sum of money. Some people claimed that in exchange for the money, Monroe promised to use his power to help the bank. A second problem came about when the time neared for Monroe to leave office. The Federalist Party no longer existed. Republicans began to argue about who should be the next president. There were four possible candidates. Sometimes congressmen ignored what Monroe said and asked advice from the men who would run for president in 1824.

James Monroe did, however, have one major success in his second term. In 1823, Monroe and his secretary of state, John Quincy Adams, wrote the Monroe **Doctrine.** Americans sympathized with

James Monroe (standing) and his secretary of state, John Quincy Adams (seated at far left), wanted to keep Europeans from interfering with new countries in the Americas. They drafted the Monroe Doctrine, which promised to stop Europeans from starting new settlements in the Western Hemisphere.

After he left the presidency, James Monroe sold Highland and moved to a property called Oak Hill, where he built this house. The Monroes hosted many famous guests there, including the Marquis de Lafayette and John Quincy Adams.

Spanish colonies in South America that fought their own revolutions. In order to demonstrate this support, the government issued this important statement. It said that the United States would not allow Europe to set up any new colonies on the American continents— on North or South America. The nation promised to protect its neighbors from any European country that tried to do so. Americans praised the Doctrine. It made little impact at the time in Europe. However, later presidents would refer to the Doctrine when making decisions as to how to deal with European countries.

In 1825, Monroe's second term ended. He was 66 years old. In his lifetime, he had already seen a great deal of change. The American colonies had become not only a free country, but a very strong country. Its territory stretched much farther across the continent.

Monroe (circled) went to Richmond, Virginia, to help write a new constitution for the state. His friend James Madison, shown here speaking to the delegates, was also at the convention.

As president, James Monroe made two goodwill tours. This meant he traveled around the United States to meet Americans. On his first trip, he went as far north as Maine and as far west as Michigan. On his second, he traveled south to Georgia and west to Missouri. He came back through Kentucky.

There were new territories and states in the West. Monroe's efforts had played a role in America's success. The lives of the American people were changing, too. When Monroe began his career in politics, most Americans still lived and worked on farms. By the time his presidency ended, many factories had opened in the United States.

After he retired, Monroe had problems to deal with in his own life. By this time, he had many debts. During his political career, the government never gave him a big salary. There had been little time to run his farm. In 1826, a year after his presidency, Monroe had to sell Highland. He and Elizabeth moved to another property that they called Oak Hill.

Monroe remained busy. He helped run the University of Virginia. He was president of the convention formed to write a new state constitution for

Virginia. He also supported the American Colonization Society. This organization established the nation of Liberia in Africa for free blacks. The country's capital was named Monrovia in his honor.

Elizabeth Monroe died in 1830. Monroe missed her very much. One year later, he died as well. The date was the fourth of July. Monroe died on the anniversary of the day America first declared its independence.

When the news of Monroe's death spread across the United States, Americans were very sad. They remembered how hard he had worked to protect the country. They knew he was responsible for much of its new territory. Americans thanked him for the strong, growing nation he had helped to create.

Monroe died on July 4, 1831, exactly five years after the deaths of Presidents Jefferson and Adams. Three of the first five presidents died on Independence Day.

The Monroe Doctrine was not called that until long after James Monroe died.

Today people visit Ash Lawn-Highland, the plantation Monroe built, to learn more about what it was like to live during his lifetime. Actors dress in costumes of the day and tell stories about life on a plantation.

THE MONROE DOCTRINE

In the early 1800s, European colonies in South America started their own wars of independence. Like the United States had done years before, they were trying to win freedom from the European countries that governed them. Some of these nations won their freedom, and James Monroe supported them. He thought they deserved to be independent nations.

He felt so strongly about it that he and his secretary of state, John Quincy Adams, created the Monroe Doctrine. This was a statement to the world about U.S. power in the Western Hemisphere, the part of the world made up by the American continents, shown in the map above.

The Monroe Doctrine said that the governments in the New World should be democratic, not ruled by kings, queens, or emperors. It promised that the United States would not bother colonies that European countries still had in the Western Hemisphere. But it also said "The American continents… are henceforth not to be considered as subjects for future colonization by any European powers." In other words, the United States would not let European powers establish any new colonies there. If any tried to do so, the United States would view it as dangerous to its own safety. For that reason, it promised to protect any country in the Americas from European attack.

Monroe is said to have used this desk when he wrote the Monroe Doctrine.

Time Line

1758
James Monroe is born on April 28 at his parents' farm in Westmoreland County, Virginia.

1769
Monroe enrolls in school for the first time. Before this, his parents taught him at home.

1774
When Monroe's father dies, Monroe inherits the estate. His uncle helps him make decisions about how to run the farm and how to spend money. Monroe attends school at the College of William and Mary in Williamsburg.

1775
Monroe and other students are angry about how England is treating the colonies. They join the local militia of volunteer soldiers.

1776
Monroe leaves college to join the Continental Army. He is wounded at the Battle of Trenton.

1780
Monroe resigns from the army and begins to study law with Thomas Jefferson.

1781
The Revolution comes to an end. The United States wins its independence.

1782
Monroe is elected to Virginia's legislature.

1783
Monroe is elected to the U.S. Congress, which meets in Philadelphia.

1785
The nation's capital moves to New York City. Members of Congress, including Monroe, move there.

1786
James Monroe marries Elizabeth Kortright on February 16. They move to Virginia. Monroe works as a lawyer.

1787
Monroe is elected to Virginia's legislature again. He holds the position until 1789.

1788
Monroe is a member of the Virginia convention that will decide whether to ratify the U.S. Constitution.

1790
Monroe is elected to the U.S. Senate.

1793
Monroe purchases his plantation, which he calls Highland.

1794
President George Washington asks Monroe to leave the Senate and become the U.S. diplomat to France. The Monroes and their firstborn child move to Paris, the capital of France.

1799
After being fired from his post in France, Monroe and his family return to the United States. He is elected governor of Virginia three years in a row.

1803
President Thomas Jefferson asks Monroe to go on a special mission to France. There Monroe helps negotiate the Louisiana Purchase. From France, Monroe will go to Spain and England as a diplomat.

1807
Monroe returns to the United States. Some Americans want him to run for president, but he does not get his political party's nomination. He goes back to Virginia.

1811
Monroe again becomes governor of Virginia. Soon after, President James Madison names Monroe his secretary of state.

1812
War breaks out between the United States and Great Britain.

1814
James Madison names Monroe the secretary of war in addition to his post as secretary of state. In August, the British attack the presidential mansion, the Capitol, and other government buildings. The war finally ends on December 24 when the two nations sign a treaty, although fighting continues until word reaches soldiers in the United States.

1816
James Monroe is elected the fifth president of the United States.

1817
Monroe is inaugurated. The "Era of Good Feeling" begins.

1818
General Andrew Jackson leads the First Seminole War, eventually seizing eastern Florida from Spain.

1819
The Adams-Onís Treaty makes East Florida part of the United States. In return, the United States gives up its claims on Texas and pays $5 million of Spanish debt.

1820
The Missouri Compromise is enacted on March 3. The Monroes' younger daughter, Maria Hester, becomes the first daughter of a president to get married at the White House. Monroe is reelected as president.

1821
Monroe begins his second term.

1823
Monroe issues the Monroe Doctrine. This statement says that the United States will not allow Europe to set up new colonies or interfere with countries in the Western Hemisphere.

1825
When Monroe's second term as president ends, he and Elizabeth leave Washington, D.C.

1826
The Monroes sell Highland plantation.

1829
Monroe is the president of the Virginia Constitutional Convention, which creates a new state constitution.

1830
Elizabeth Monroe dies on September 23. Monroe goes to New York City to live with his daughter, Maria Hester.

1831
James Monroe dies on July 4, exactly five years after the deaths of presidents Jefferson and Adams.

G L O S S A R Y

ally (AL-lie) An ally is a nation that has agreed to help another nation, for example, by fighting together against a common enemy. Some Americans wanted the United States to become an English ally.

ammunition (am-yuh-NISH-en) Ammunition is bullets, cannonballs, and other things that can be exploded or fired from guns. The Americans began to stockpile ammunition before the American Revolution began.

compromise (KOM-pruh-myz) A compromise is a way to settle a disagreement in which both sides give up part of what they want. The Missouri Compromise made Maine a free state and Missouri a slave state.

constitution (kon-stih-TOO-shun) A constitution is the set of basic principles that govern a state, country, or society. The states sent delegates to help write a new constitution for the United States.

convention (kun-VEN-shun) A convention is a large meeting. Delegates at the Constitutional Convention gathered to write the U.S. constitution.

debt (DET) Debt is something that is owed to someone, especially money. In the Adams-Onís Treaty, the United States agreed to pay $5 million worth of Spanish debt.

delegates (DEL-eh-getz) Delegates are people elected to take part in something. Delegates from each state met at the Constitutional Convention.

democracy (deh-MOK-ruh-see) A democracy is a country in which the government is run by the people who live there. The United States is a democracy.

diplomat (DIP-luh-mat) A diplomat is a government official whose job is to represent a country in discussions with other countries. The U.S. government sent Monroe to France as a diplomat.

doctrine (DOK-trin) A doctrine is something that a nation, religion, or other group firmly believes. The Monroe Doctrine stated that the United States had the right to stop any European country from trying to colonize the Americas.

electoral votes (ee-LEKT-uh-rul VOTZ) Electoral votes are votes cast by representatives of the American public for the president and vice president. Each state chooses representatives who vote for a candidate in an election. These representatives vote according to what the majority of people in their state want.

foreign affairs (FOR-un uh-FAIRZ) Foreign affairs are matters involving other countries. Monroe is best known for his achievements in foreign affairs.

inaugural address (ih-NAW-gyuh-rul uh-DRESS) An inaugural address is the speech an elected president makes at his or her inauguration, the ceremony that takes place when a new president begins a term. Monroe gave his first inaugural address in 1817.

inherited (in-HAIR-ih-tid) If a person inherited something, he or she received it when someone else died. When his father died, James inherited all his father's money and land.

landslide (LAND-slyd) If a candidate wins an election by a landslide, he or she wins by a huge number of votes. Monroe won his second election by a landslide.

legislature (LEJ-eh-slay-chur) A legislature is the group of people who make laws for a state or country. Monroe was elected to Virginia's legislature in 1782 and 1787.

mentor (MEN-tor) A mentor is someone who is a trusted counselor to another person, often offering advice about important things. Thomas Jefferson was James Monroe's mentor.

militia (meh-LISH-uh) A militia is a volunteer army, made up of citizens who have trained as soldiers. Monroe joined Virginia's militia before the Revolution.

minister (MIN-uh-stur) A minister is a person who represents one country in another country. Monroe was the U.S. minister to France.

mission (MISH-un) A mission is when a person is sent someplace for a special purpose. Monroe went on a special mission to France.

negotiate (nee-GOH-she-ayt) If people negotiate, they talk things over and try to come to an agreement. Monroe helped negotiate the Louisiana Purchase.

neutral (NOO-trul) If people are neutral, they do not take sides. President Washington believed the United States should be neutral and not get involved in problems between other nations.

plantation (plan-TAY-shun) A plantation is a large farm or group of farms that grows crops such as tobacco, sugarcane, or cotton. Monroe's plantation was called Highland.

political parties (puh-LIT-uh-kul PAR-teez) Political parties are groups of people who share similar ideas about how to run a government. Monroe belonged to the Democratic-Republican political party.

politics (PAWL-uh-tiks) Politics refers to the actions and practices of the government. After the Revolution, Monroe began his career in politics.

promoted (pruh-MOHT-id) If someone is promoted, he or she receives a more important job or position. The army promoted Monroe to recognize his bravery.

rebellion (reh-BEL-yen) A rebellion is a fight against one's government. Monroe heard other colonists talk about a rebellion when he was very young.

representative (rep-ree-ZEN-tuh-tiv) A representative is someone who attends a meeting, having agreed to speak or act for others. American colonists wanted a representative in England's government.

revolution (rev-uh-LOO-shun) A revolution is something that causes a complete change in government. The American Revolution was a war fought between the United States and Great Britain.

secretary of state (SEK-ruh-tair-ee OF STAYT) The secretary of state is a close advisor to the president. He or she is involved in the nation's relations with other countries.

surveyors (sur-VAY-urz) Surveyors are people who determine the boundaries of a piece of land. In Monroe's day, surveyors made maps and measured pieces of property.

taxes (TAK-sez) Taxes are sums of money paid by people to support the government and its services. American colonists did not want to pay taxes to England if they did not have a representative in government.

term (TERM) A term of office is the length of time politicians can keep their positions by law. Monroe's first term in Congress ended in 1786.

treaty (TREE-tee) A treaty is a formal agreement between nations. The Adams-Onís Treaty gave East Florida to the United States.

THE UNITED STATES GOVERNMENT

The United States government is divided into three equal branches: the executive, the legislative, and the judicial. This division helps prevent abuses of power because each branch has to answer to the other two. No one branch can become too powerful.

EXECUTIVE BRANCH

PRESIDENT
VICE PRESIDENT
DEPARTMENTS

The job of the executive branch is to enforce the laws. It is headed by the president, who serves as the spokesperson for the United States around the world. The president signs bills into law and appoints important officials such as federal judges. He or she is also the commander in chief of the U.S. military. The president is assisted by the vice president, who takes over if the president dies or cannot carry out the duties of the office.

The executive branch also includes various departments, each focused on a specific topic. They include the Defense Department, the Justice Department, and the Agriculture Department. The department heads, along with other officials such as the vice president, serve as the president's closest advisers, called the cabinet.

LEGISLATIVE BRANCH

CONGRESS
Senate and
House of Representatives

The job of the legislative branch is to make the laws. It consists of Congress, which is divided into two parts: the Senate and the House of Representatives. The Senate has 100 members, and the House of Representatives has 435 members. Each state has two senators. The number of representatives a state has varies depending on the state's population.

Besides making laws, Congress also passes budgets and enacts taxes. In addition, it is responsible for declaring war, maintaining the military, and regulating trade with other countries.

JUDICIAL BRANCH

SUPREME COURT
COURTS OF APPEALS
DISTRICT COURTS

The job of the judicial branch is to interpret the laws. It consists of the nation's federal courts. Trials are held in district courts. During trials, judges must decide what laws mean and how they apply. Courts of appeals review the decisions made in district courts.

The nation's highest court is the Supreme Court. If someone disagrees with a court of appeals ruling, he or she can ask the Supreme Court to review it. The Supreme Court may refuse. The Supreme Court makes sure that decisions and laws do not violate the Constitution.

CHOOSING
THE PRESIDENT

It may seem odd, but American voters don't elect the president directly. Instead, the president is chosen using what is called the Electoral College.

Each state gets as many votes in the Electoral College as its combined total of senators and representatives in Congress. For example, Iowa has two senators and five representatives, so it gets seven electoral votes. Although the District of Columbia does not have any voting members in Congress, it gets three electoral votes. Usually, the candidate who wins the most votes in any given state receives all of that state's electoral votes.

To become president, a candidate must get more than half of the Electoral College votes. There are a total of 538 votes in the Electoral College, so a candidate needs 270 votes to win. If nobody receives 270 Electoral College votes, the House of Representatives chooses the president.

With the Electoral College system, the person who receives the most votes nationwide does not always receive the most electoral votes. This happened most recently in 2000, when Al Gore received half a million more national votes than George W. Bush. Bush became president because he had more Electoral College votes.

THE WHITE HOUSE

The White House is the official home of the president of the United States. It is located at 1600 Pennsylvania Avenue NW in Washington, D.C. In 1792, a contest was held to select the architect who would design the president's home. James Hoban won. Construction took eight years.

The first president, George Washington, never lived in the White House. The second president, John Adams, moved into the house in 1800, though the inside was not yet complete. During the War of 1812, British soldiers burned down much of the White House. It was rebuilt several years later.

The White House was changed through the years. Porches were added, and President Theodore Roosevelt added the West Wing. President William Taft changed the shape of the presidential office, making it into the famous Oval Office. While Harry Truman was president, the old house was discovered to be structurally weak. All the walls were reinforced with steel, and the rooms were rebuilt.

Today, the White House has 132 rooms (including 35 bathrooms), 28 fireplaces, and 3 elevators. It takes 570 gallons of paint to cover the outside of the six-story building. The White House provides the president with many ways to relax. It includes a putting green, a jogging track, a swimming pool, a tennis court, and beautifully landscaped gardens. The White House also has a movie theater, a billiard room, and a one-lane bowling alley.

PRESIDENTIAL PERKS

The job of president of the United States is challenging. It is probably one of the most stressful jobs in the world. Because of this, presidents are paid well, though not nearly as well as the leaders of large corporations. In 2007, the president earned $400,000 a year. Presidents also receive extra benefits that make the demanding job a little more appealing.

★ **Camp David:** In the 1940s, President Franklin D. Roosevelt chose this heavily wooded spot in the mountains of Maryland to be the presidential retreat, where presidents can relax. Even though it is a retreat, world business is conducted there. Most famously, President Jimmy Carter met with Middle Eastern leaders at Camp David in 1978. The result was a peace agreement between Israel and Egypt.

★ *Air Force One*: The president flies on a jet called *Air Force One*. It is a Boeing 747-200B that has been modified to meet the president's needs.

Air Force One is the size of a large home. It is equipped with a dining room, sleeping quarters, a conference room, and office space. It also has two kitchens that can provide food for up to 50 people.

★ **The Secret Service:** While not the most glamorous of the president's perks, the Secret Service is one of the most important. The Secret Service is a group of highly trained agents who protect the president and the president's family.

★ **The Presidential State Car:** The presidential limousine is a stretch Cadillac DTS.

It has been armored to protect the president in case of attack. Inside the plush car are a foldaway desk, an entertainment center, and a communications console.

★ **The Food:** The White House has five chefs who will make any food the president wants. The White House also has an extensive wine collection.

★ **Retirement:** A former president receives a pension, or retirement pay, of just under $180,000 a year. Former presidents also receive Secret Service protection for the rest of their lives.

FACTS

QUALIFICATIONS

To run for president, a candidate must

- ★ be at least 35 years old
- ★ be a citizen who was born in the United States
- ★ have lived in the United States for 14 years

TERM OF OFFICE

A president's term of office is four years.
No president can stay in office for more than two terms.

ELECTION DATE

The presidential election takes place every four years on the first Tuesday of November.

INAUGURATION DATE

Presidents are inaugurated on January 20.

OATH OF OFFICE

I do solemnly swear I will faithfully execute the office of the President of the United States and will to the best of my ability preserve, protect, and defend the Constitution of the United States.

WRITE A LETTER TO THE PRESIDENT

One of the best things about being a U.S. citizen is that Americans get to participate in their government. They can speak out if they feel government leaders aren't doing their jobs. They can also praise leaders who are going the extra mile. Do you have something you'd like the president to do? Should the president worry more about the environment and encourage people to recycle? Should the government spend more money on our schools? You can write a letter to the president to say how you feel!

1600 Pennsylvania Avenue
Washington, D.C. 20500
You can even send an e-mail to: president@whitehouse.gov

BOOKS

Hakim, Joy. *From Colonies to Country.* New York: Oxford University Press, 1993.

Kelley, Brent. *James Monroe: American Statesman.* Philadelphia: Chelsea House, 2001.

Robinet, Harriette Gillem. *Washington City Is Burning.* New York: Atheneum, 1996.

Santella, Andrew. *James Monroe: America's 5th President.* New York: Children's Press, 2003.

VIDEOS

The American President. DVD, VHS (Alexandria, VA: PBS Home Video, 2000).

The History Channel Presents The Presidents. DVD (New York: A & E Home Video, 2005).

The History Channel Presents The War of 1812. DVD (New York: A & E Home Video, 2004).

National Geographic's Inside the White House. DVD (Washington, D.C.: National Geographic Video, 2003).

INTERNET SITES

Visit our Web page for lots of links about James Monroe and other U.S. presidents:

http://www.childsworld.com/links

Note to Parents, Teachers, and Librarians: We routinely verify our Web links to make sure they are safe, active sites—so encourage your readers to check them out!

INDEX